FLAGLER'S ST. AUGUSTINE HOTELS

Tommy Thompson/Flagler College Archives

FLAGLER'S ST. AUGUSTINE HOTELS

THE PONCE DE LEON, THE ALCAZAR, AND THE CASA MONICA

Thomas Graham

PINEAPPLE PRESS, INC.

SARASOTA, FLORIDA

Inquiries should be addressed to:

Pineapple Press, Inc.
P.O. Box 3889
Sarasota, Florida 34230

www.pineapplepress.com

Library of Congress Cataloging-in-Publication Data

Graham, Thomas, 1943–
  Flagler's St. Augustine hotels : the Ponce de Leon, the Alcazar, and the Casa Monica / Thomas Graham.— 1st ed.
       p. cm.
Includes bibliographical references and index.
  ISBN 1-56164-300-9 (pbk. : alk. paper)
  1. Hotels—Florida—Saint Augustine—History. I. Title.
  TX909.G73 2004
  917.59'18—dc22
                                                          2003020976

First Edition
10 9 8 7 6 5 4 3 2 1

Design by Shé Heaton
Printed in China

—

TABLE OF CONTENTS

ACKNOWLEDGMENTS

The author wishes to thank the staff of the Henry Morrison Flagler Museum in Palm Beach for their help in the research that went into this book. The Flagler Museum is the primary repository for materials relating to the life and career of Henry M. Flagler. The librarians of the St. Augustine Historical Society also deserve a great deal of my gratitude for their assistance in locating documents and photographs from the Flagler era of St. Augustine's history. Finally, I owe great thanks to the staff of the Flagler College Office of Institutional Advancement, the custodians of the college's small archive of photographs and other memorabilia related to the Hotel Ponce de Leon.

INTRODUCTION

For a few brief years near the conclusion of the nineteenth century, St. Augustine became the ultimate winter resort for the social and financial elite of the United States. America's oldest city seemed destined to develop into the nation's "Winter Newport." That dream briefly became reality, but then the Ancient City was quickly left behind in the Florida frontier's rush southward down the Atlantic Coast. A grand design, started in St. Augustine, ended with the creation of Palm Beach and Miami—and modern Florida.

Remaining today in St. Augustine as enduring monuments to the city's moment of brilliance are a collection of magnificent buildings. Chief among these are the hotels of Henry Morrison Flagler: the Ponce de Leon, Alcazar, and Casa Monica. These buildings are the creations of preeminent American architects and artists. Although they echo the architecture of Renaissance Spain, their builders employed forward-looking innovations in construction and building materials. They were the first large buildings in the United States made of concrete.

Built more than a century ago, these hotels still preside over the city's skyline. The hotels are landmarks in the rise of Florida's tourist industry, but they are also, in themselves, unique national treasures of architecture and art. In modern times, they also give testimony to the creative adaptation of historic structures to new uses in a vibrant, living city.

The towers of the Hotel Ponce de Leon, today Flagler College, have dominated the skyline of St. Augustine for more than a century.

HENRY MORRISON FLAGLER

Henry Morrison Flagler, author of the plan to make St. Augustine the Winter Newport, came from that class of "new money" millionaires created by the rise of big business. Like a hero of the day's dime novels, Flagler made his fortune through pluck and hard work. Born the son of a modest Presbyterian minister in western New York in 1830, he moved to Ohio as a boy. With the help of relatives, he went on to accumulate a small fortune in the grain trade. During the Civil War, he ventured to Michigan and plunged his wealth into salt mining, only to lose it all. After the war, he returned to Ohio, where he went into the newfangled business of refining oil in partnership with an old acquaintance, John D. Rockefeller.

Henry Morrison Flagler

Flagler and Rockefeller became close business partners and good friends. They shared the same office, and they lived near each other on Euclid Avenue in Cleveland's most fashionable neighborhood. They often walked to and from the office together, talking business along the way. Their firm quickly grew to become Standard Oil, one of the giants of world business enterprise. Later on, Rockefeller was asked if he had originated the concept of Standard Oil Trust. He replied, "No, sir. I wish I'd had the brains to think of it. It was Henry M. Flagler." By the 1880s, Rockefeller and Flagler had migrated along with the company headquarters to New York City, the emerging financial capital of the world. They occupied adjoining townhouses just off Fifth Avenue. Both partners had amassed personal fortunes that ranked them among the richest men on earth.

Years later, when Flagler was asked how he came to embark on his Florida enterprises, the taciturn millionaire replied, "Oh, it's just one of those things that just happen. I happened to be in St. Augustine and had some spare money." This answer is true, as far as it goes, but it doesn't explain how he made his way to St. Augustine, and it understates the planning that stood behind his decision to

10

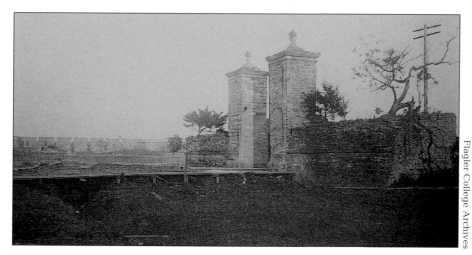

Flagler College Archives

*St. Augustine City Gate. Noted photographer Edward Bierstadt
recorded views of St. Augustine in 1891 for a book sold by the
Cordova Hotel's "El Unico" gift shop.*

turn away from Standard Oil and become the entrepreneurial patron of half a state.

Flagler first came to Florida in the late 1870s because of the deteriorating health of his frail first wife, Mary. The long trip south by railroad and steamship was a physically wearing ordeal. They stayed in Jacksonville but, like many winter visitors, took a side trip by steamboat up the St. Johns River and then overland by the short St. Johns Railroad from Tocoi to St. Augustine. At the time, St. Augustine was noted for its rustic, Spanish antiquity and was known as a warm-weather refuge for invalids from the North. Flagler regret-

ted making the excursion. "I did not form a very favorable first impression, I must admit. I came here from Jacksonville by way of the river and the Tocoi Railway and got here just at night. The accommodation was very bad, and most of the visitors here were consumptives. I didn't like it and took the first train back to Jacksonville."

Flagler returned to New York and put Florida out of his mind. Then, in 1881, Mary died, and both Flagler's business life and personal life took some dramatic turns. He began to withdraw gradually from the daily affairs of Standard Oil—which, after all, really was Rockefeller's company—and started

11

searching for some new individual enterprise to throw himself into. In the summer of 1883, he married Ida Alice Shourds, a red-haired, blue-eyed beauty who had attended Mary during her years of declining health. "Alicia," as she called herself, was thirty-five and Flagler was fifty-three, an age difference not all that exceptional in the Victorian era. The following winter, he took her on a belated honeymoon to Florida. Flagler also thought the change in climate might improve his "disorderly liver." He had not planned on returning to St. Augustine but went on his doctor's advice.

Arriving again in the Ancient City, Flagler was surprised to discover a "wonderful change." Most sojourners in town were not the pathetic consumptives he remembered from his first visit but "that class of society one meets at the great watering places of Europe— men who go there to enjoy themselves and not for the benefit of their health." Pleased with the improvement, the Flaglers returned a year later, in February 1885, for another stay in the large new San Marco Hotel, which had just recently been completed and stood north of the City Gate across from the old Spanish fort. The San Marco repre-

Flagler College Archives

San Marco Hotel, where Flagler stayed before he built his own hotels.

sented a landmark improvement in the quality of accommodations in the town. Nevertheless, Flagler still found St. Augustine a "dull place."

I liked it well enough to stay, and since I couldn't sit still all the time, I used daily to take the walks down St. George Street, around the plaza to the club house, and back to the hotel again. I found that all the other gentlemen did the same thing, with the same apparent regularity and then, as now, that was all there was to do for recreation and amusement.

But I liked the place and the climate, and it occurred to me very strongly that someone with sufficient means ought to provide accommodations for the class of people who are not sick, but who come here to enjoy the climate, and have plenty of money, but could find no satisfactory way of spending it.

While he was in St. Augustine, Flagler, along with the rest of the winter visitors, witnessed the annual Ponce de León Celebration.

Flagler College Archives

Artist Frank Shapleigh, who occupied one of the Hotel Ponce de Leon studios, painted this picture of Hypolita Street with its orange tree and Spanish moss–covered oak.

"Explorers" dressed in sixteenth-century Spanish costume landed at the city dock in a small barge modified to resemble a Spanish galleon flying a limp sail. For the next three days, schools and businesses closed as the town's bankers, clerks, shopkeepers, and tradesmen thronged the streets in the guise of Indians, Frenchmen, Spaniards, and pirates. Baseball games, sailing regattas, band concerts, and dances filled out the festivities. It was quite an event for a town of fewer than three thousand souls.

Three centuries earlier, Juan Ponce de León had come to Florida as the middle-aged former governor of Puerto Rico, searching for new worlds to conquer—and perhaps for the legendary Fountain of Youth. Like that renowned explorer, Flagler landed in St. Augustine seeking new challenges, new enterprises, and a renewed start on life. A plan began to form in his mind: Build a first-class hotel, some places of amusement, a modern railroad connection to the North—and St. Augustine could become the American Riviera.

The typical overhanging balconies of St. Augustine's houses inspired Flagler's architects who designed the Hotel Ponce de Leon.

THE PONCE DE LEON

As Flagler pondered the challenges of turning St. Augustine into the Winter Newport, he began trying out some of these ideas on a gentleman with whom he had struck up an acquaintance: upper-crust Boston philanthropist Franklin W. Smith, one of the founders of the YMCA. A seasoned world traveler and amateur architect, Smith was brimming with his own visions for developing St. Augustine and filling it with new buildings reproducing the architecture of ancient Egypt, Greece, and Rome. Smith's own winter home set an example of what he had in mind. His Villa Zorayda was an exotic amalgam borrowing from Spain's Moorish castles, but the most unusual and

Franklin W. Smith's home Villa Zorayda was the first modern concrete building erected in St. Augustine.

important feature of Smith's home was its cast-in-place concrete walls. This was an old building technique that employed a brand new material: Portland cement. Concrete construction itself was not new. Long before, the ancient Romans had built massive concrete temples and stadiums, and later the humble Spanish colonists in St. Augustine had erected walls of *tapia,* "tabby," made from a mixture of oyster shell, sand, and lime. But Portland cement opened the way for much more sophisticated modern uses of concrete, and, in St. Augustine, it would be cheaper than brick imported from the North and more durable than wood.

Flagler and Smith agreed on a deal to build a $200,000 hotel, with Smith doing most of the work and Flagler, as silent partner, supplying most of the financing. This arrangement quickly proved unworkable. For one thing, Smith could not come up with his share of the financing. Also, one suspects that Flagler, who was accustomed to getting his way, could not get along comfortably with the equally strong-willed Smith. As often happened with his later Florida enterprises, Flagler found that his original plan lured him into much greater commitments than he had first contemplated. One thing led to another.

Flagler discussed his vision with the manager of the San Marco Hotel, Osburn D. Seavey, whom he soon hired to serve as an expert consultant and even-

16

tually manager of his hotel. Seavey, a stocky, blue-eyed Yankee with a full, blond beard, looked like the ideal innkeeper. Another key strategist, Dr. Andrew Anderson, joined the conversations. He owned an orange grove at the western edge of town, which he offered as the site for the proposed hotel. But Dr. Anderson was much more than just an important property owner. His family had come to St. Augustine from New York City a generation earlier, he still maintained strong New York connections, and he had become one of the most influential men in town. Soon he would be mayor. Flagler found Dr. Anderson a congenial personality, and their relationship developed into a warm, lifelong friendship.

Flagler would later say that originating the design for the Hotel Ponce de Leon was the most perplexing task he ever faced in his Florida enterprises: "Here was St. Augustine, the oldest city in the United States. How to build a hotel to meet the requirements of nineteenth-century America and have it in keeping with the character of the place—that was my hardest problem."

Returning to New York, Flagler hit upon a bold gamble in choosing the architects for his hotels. Thomas Hastings, the son of Flagler's Presbyterian minister, possessed a flair for creating fanciful architectural designs, and the young Hastings had already done a few small projects for Flagler. According to John Carrère, Hastings' twenty-six-year-old colleague: "We and our sole assistant, an office boy, were sitting in our office waiting for something to turn up" when Flagler summoned Hastings. Hours later, he returned with a banging of doors, shouting, "We are going to Florida! We've got a million-dollar hotel to build there!" Hastings and Carrère and their office boy then proceeded to smash everything breakable in their office in a delirious celebration.

In May 1885, Flagler brought Hastings and a New York real estate expert to St. Augustine in his private railroad car to assess the situation. Hastings spent the train trip sketching visionary designs for the hotel. Once in St. Augustine, the party joined Dr. Anderson at his home, Markland, and the planning sessions continued in the

Markland, home of Flagler's friend Dr. Andrew Anderson.

doctor's parlor long into the succeeding nights. Dr. Anderson was assigned the task of purchasing, as quietly as possible, all the land necessary for the hotel.

Hastings' first visit to the proposed site of the hotel was a sobering experience. After a short walk through Dr. Anderson's orange grove, they arrived at the place. "When Mr. Flagler led me to the spot where he wanted the Ponce de Leon to stand, I was discouraged for it was low and marshy, in fact, a continuation of Maria Sanchez Creek." The only buildings on the site were a

Methodist Church, a roller-skating rink, and the modest Sunnyside Hotel. All stood on pilings, with tidal waters flowing beneath them. Flagler reassured Hastings that plans were under way to remove the existing buildings and fill the whole Maria Sanchez basin. Despite the site's forlorn appearance, it was a large, contiguous tract that could be developed any way Hastings' imagination and Flagler's money would take it.

While in St. Augustine, Hastings inspected the town's curious old houses. "I spent much time roaming around St.

18

Workers prepare to fill Maria Sanchez Creek and remove the skating rink (left) and Olivet Methodist Church to make way for Flagler's hotels.

Augustine endeavoring to absorb as much of the local atmosphere as possible. I wanted to retain the Spanish character of St. Augustine and so designed the buildings with architecture of the early houses here with their quaint overhanging balconies."

Both Hastings and Carrère were familiar with Spanish architecture. Born in 1860, Hastings had studied at the École des Beaux-Arts in Paris, where he met Carrère. While in Europe, Hastings traveled in Spain to study the architectural traditions of that country. John Carrère had been born in Rio de Janeiro, the son of an American coffee planter. Thus Carrère grew up amid Iberian architecture. "Yet," Hastings later declared, "it was not so much our predilections for Spanish architecture as our conscientious scruples against destroying the characteristic atmosphere of St. Augustine that guided us. . . . We realized that by putting up an incongruous structure we might destroy the individuality and charm of the old Spanish community." In retrospect, the choice of a Spanish Renaissance style seems natural, but it was a new departure in American architecture at the time.

The Flagler party also examined the concrete walls of Villa Zorayda and crossed the bay to the quarries on Anastasia Island to study the coquina

19

Artist Frank Shapleigh's rendition of the old Spanish Castillo de San Marcos, which the U. S. Army called Fort Marion in Flagler's day.

shell that had been used as the aggregate in the Zorayda's concrete mix. Coquina is the shell of a tiny mollusk that lives on Florida beaches. Thick deposits exist on Anastasia Island, some in the form of loose shell and some compressed over thousands of years into solid layers of stone. The Spanish had used the hard shell stone in their fort and buildings; Flagler needed the loose shell. Hastings, showing he understood the concept that a building needed to grow from its environment, commented that coquina "was a suggestion of nature not to be overlooked."

Returning to New York, Carrère devoted himself primarily to the business side of the project, while Hastings handled the artistic aspects. "We made more elaborate perspective drawings and studies and plans, but gradually transferred these drawings into more practical working drawings, finally figuring the plans. These plans were intricate in outline, and

Flagler College Archives

Flagler laid temporary railways on St. Augustine's streets to haul in building materials for the Hotel Ponce de Leon.

for a building covering somewhat over six acres of ground," Hastings wrote.

Meanwhile, Flagler hired Frederick Bruce, the only licensed civil engineer in the area, to plan and execute the filling of the marsh. Bruce was superintendent of Fort Marion, as the U.S. Army called the old Spanish castle. Bruce arranged for temporary railroad tracks to be laid down on the streets to haul in sand from north of town.

Actual construction of Flagler's hotel was entrusted to James A. McGuire and Joseph McDonald, the men who had built Seavey's San Marco Hotel. McGuire and McDonald were New Englanders who started out as shipbuilders and then constructed conventional pine-wood hotels in Florida. McGuire was a giant of a man, standing six foot six, who had little for-

21

mal schooling but lots of experience and natural intuition about how to construct buildings. McGuire and McDonald would spend months experimenting and performing tests on concrete structural elements to determine their load-bearing capabilities. For the most part, their concrete buildings stood only on the strength of their thick walls, but critical points, such as corners and the spaces above arches, were reinforced with steel I-beams or lengths of railroad track. McGuire and McDonald thought about using concrete in the interior flooring but settled on old-fashioned Southern heart pine, which itself approaches the hardness of steel, for the floors and interior wall framing.

When McGuire and McDonald began marking out the

The roof of the Hotel Ponce de Leon's dining room is being framed out, while on the right wooden forms hold another pour of concrete to raise the walls of the hotel's utility wing.

outline of the hotel from the blueprints Carrère and Hastings had shipped down, they found that the figures did not work out properly. So Hastings made a hurried visit to St. Augustine to straighten out matters, and from then on Carrère and Hastings became full-fledged partners in the hotel's construction. They were the New York contractors for building materials for the hotel.

Work commenced on the hotel on December 1, 1885, with a crowd of citizens watching the ceremonial turning of the first spadeful of dirt. The massive foundations were poured with an especially strong mixture of Portland cement. Flagler commented philosophically, "I think it more likely I am spending an unnecessary amount of money in the foundation walls, but I comfort myself with the reflection that a hundred years hence it will be all the same to me, and the building the better because of my extravagance."

Liquid concrete from great, steam-powered cement mixers was hauled up to wooden forms, poured into troughs, and tamped into place by some of the seven hundred laborers who had moved into town to work on the building. Each pour was about eighteen inches thick. After allowing the concrete to cure for several days, workers removed the wooden forms, reassembled them at the next higher level, and poured another course of concrete. Flagler fretted about delays and tried to hurry the work along so the hotel could open on January 1, 1887, but that deadline passed and the hotel was not completed until May—too late for that winter's tourist season.

While the hotel's walls were rising, Flagler busied himself perfecting plans to make sure his resort hotel venture would be a success. He purchased the railroad connecting St. Augustine to Jacksonville, converted it to standard gauge, and constructed a bridge across the St. Johns River to link up with railroads running north. Thereafter, guests could leave gray, frozen New York in a plush Pullman palace car and arrive in the Land of Flowers thirty-five hours later. The trip to Florida became a pleasure tour rather than the torturous ordeal it had been before. Thousands of copies of *Florida, The American Riviera*, an illustrated guide to the Hotel Ponce de

The world gained its first glimpse of the Hotel Ponce de Leon from sketches in the promotional book Florida, the American Riviera.

Leon's wonders, were distributed to notables in America and Europe to make certain the world would know what was about to happen in the nation's oldest city.

Interest in the North rose to a high level. Flagler was well known from his years with Standard Oil, and anything with which he involved himself became news. Some were skeptical of his Florida enterprise. The stony-faced businessman revealed a sense of wry humor in his reply to the curious:

> I have two stories to tell to every one who asks me my rea-
> sons for building the Ponce de Leon Hotel. . . . I was coming
> downtown in an El road car in New York recently when a
> friend said to me, "Flagler, I was asked the other day why you
> were building that hotel in St. Augustine and replied that you

had been looking around for several years for a place to make a fool of yourself in, and at last selected St. Augustine as the spot." The other story that I used to illustrate my position is this: There was once a good old church member who had always lived a correct life, until well advanced in years he got on a spree. While in this state he met his good pastor. After being roundly upbraided for his condition, he replied, "I have been giving all my days to the Lord hitherto, and now I'm taking one for myself." This is somewhat my case. For fourteen years I have devoted my time exclusively to business, and now I am pleasing myself.

There is a story that one day Flagler was walking around the construction site of his great hotel, smoking a big Havana cigar, when a security guard stopped him, told him he didn't belong there, and pointed to a "No Smoking" sign. Flagler observed that seeing as how he owned the place, he would very well go on and smoke where he pleased. The resolute watchman replied, "There have been a great many Flaglers trying to get in here lately." Just then James McGuire happened by and explained that this man really was everyone's boss. Flagler proceeded to compliment the guard for his diligence and continued on his tour, puffing on his cigar.

As the day of the Ponce de Leon's grand opening neared, an army of painters worked in shifts around the clock putting a coat of yellow paint on the hotel's wooden trim. Dozens of laborers were given severance pay and discharged. Giant bonfires of rubbish from the construction site lit up the evening sky,

The newly opened Hotel Ponce de Leon rose amid a freshly-planted landscape and carefully graded sand streets.

and schooners at the city dock unloaded asphalt to pave the sandy street from the railway depot to the hotel. Finally, the employees of the hotel—some 350 professional resort workers from the North—began arriving, their one-way train fare paid by Flagler.

The Hotel Ponce de Leon, upon its completion, had the appearance of a European castle magically transported to the shores of America and settled amid freshly laid sod lawns and newly planted palm trees. It was a large building, yet not overwhelming in bulk or extent. The structure epitomized the Beaux-Arts ideals of symmetry, proportion, and balance. The strongest lines accentuated the horizontal—as befit Florida's flat landscape—yet its central dome and the spires of its twin towers pointed toward the heavens. Carrère and Hastings called the architecture of their creation "Spanish Renaissance," and it clearly imitated that style, though they had drawn on any tradition that suited their purposes. The Hotel Ponce de Leon launched the "Mediterranean" style that has been popular in Florida ever since. At the time, it was novel—St. Augustine had not seen red barrel-tile

Murals by George W. Maynard and glass by Louis C. Tiffany grace the ceiling and walls of the Hotel Ponce de Leon's dining room.

roofs before this building.

On January 10, 1888, the first plush vestibule train ever to arrive in St. Augustine pulled into the station. Its passengers, the invited guests of Flagler, were taken to the Ponce de Leon at dusk and saw for the first time the majestic hotel glimmering with thousands of electric lights. Those taking dinner with Mr. and Mrs. Flagler that evening included the hotel's archi-

tects, builders, artists, and railroad executives. Thomas Hastings observed that turning the hotel over to manager Seavey meant that the hotel was no longer his; it was like "parting from a loved child."

Two days later, the hotel opened its register for guests. The first grand ball premiered in the large vaulted dining hall, with two orchestras playing in music lofts at both ends of the room.

Among the hundreds in attendance were Mrs. Ulysses S. Grant and Frederick Vanderbilt. Another ball later in the season attracted William R. Rockefeller. Flagler's dream of a winter vacation palace had become a reality. For the next half dozen years, the Hotel Ponce de Leon would reign as the epitome of winter resorts. It was a time when a chance meeting in the halls of the hotel might result in a conversation among Flagler, Hamilton Disston (the nation's biggest landowner), U.S. Vice President Levi P. Morton, Congressman (and later Governor) Roswell Flower of New York, Chauncey Depew (president of the New York Central Railroad), and Charles A. Dana (editor of *The New York Sun*).

In its second month, the Hotel Ponce de Leon played host to President Grover Cleveland. He arrived at the front gate of the hotel in a coach pulled by four white

President Warren G. Harding (second from left) sits with Robert Murray, manager of the Hotel Ponce de Leon. Mrs. Harding and Mrs. Murray are on the right.

horses after having threaded a circuitous route through the town's streets, past banner-decked hotel balconies and under triumphal arches of tree branches, all the while being cheered by the town's citizenry and winter visitors. In the grand parlor, he received several thousand persons, shaking hands with rich and humble, white and black. Cleveland would return to the Ponce de Leon five more times—in 1889, 1893, 1899, 1903, and 1905.

Four other presidents would enjoy the hospitality of the hotel. William McKinley, then governor of Ohio, stopped by in 1895. In October 1905, the hotel opened out of season for Theodore Roosevelt, even though the trust-busting president was no friend of Standard Oil. (Flagler's brother-in-law William R. Kenan later noted dryly that Roosevelt never thanked anyone for the pains taken to accommodate him.) Warren G. Harding enjoyed two long visits in 1921 and 1922. Harding thoroughly enjoyed himself. He fished, boated, shook hands with admiring constituents, and golfed at the Flagler links north of town (where he reportedly enjoyed some bootleg

gin). More recently, then–Vice President Lyndon B. Johnson stayed at the hotel in March 1963 when he came to town to help launch restoration of the historic St. George Street district.

In the Hotel Ponce de Leon's heyday, guests would be carried from the train depot to the front gate in a brightly painted horse-drawn omnibus. They disembarked at the medieval-style portcullis and entered a tropical garden courtyard with a decorative fountain spewing water into the air. The courtyard faced south to catch the winter sun, and on the surrounding loggias an array of green rocking chairs accommodated

Terracotta frogs surround the fountain in the courtyard of the Hotel Ponce de Leon.

guests who wished to absorb the tropical atmosphere. The carriage, meanwhile, would continue around to the back of the hotel, where huge workers—usually black men who were known as "luggage busters"—would unload the steamer trunks and whisk them to the guests' rooms by way of a freight elevator. No luggage ever marred the ambiance of the hotel rotunda.

Newly arrived visitors would look up to marvel at the overhanging balconies, the corner "Mirador Rooms," the central dome with its large copper lantern, and the twin towers that rose majestically above the flat Florida landscape. The towers held huge tanks that supplied water for the hotel—thus they were functional as well as decorative. Massive orange terra cotta balconies hung on all four sides of the towers, anchored firmly in place by railroad tracks sunk into the concrete walls. Under the dome, a glass-front solarium opened onto the roof, where potted citrus trees formed a small garden. Tin gargoyles gazed down into the courtyard, each holding an electric light bulb

Flagler College Archives

Guests at the Hotel Ponce de Leon enjoyed southern exposure on the loggias surrounding the courtyard.

in its mouth—a mixing of the old and the new that typified the hotel.

Guests entered the hotel through varnished oak doors under a mosaic archway studded with bronze scallop shells and circled with a wide band of salmon-colored terra cotta. Inside the doors, light entered only through the filter of stained-glass windows. As the visitor took his first few steps into this wondrous interior, the ceiling was low and the view ahead obscured by a row of columns. But after a few more steps forward, the guest found his gaze soaring upward to the rotunda dome with its intricate oak and plaster decorations. Persian rugs and potted palms accentuated the atmosphere. This flourish of Oriental opulence assured the jaded tourist that he wasn't in Kansas City anymore.

The murals covering the dome were the work of George W. Maynard, the country's leading artist in that specialty. The motifs employed allegorical female figures and medallions commemorating places and heroes from the pasts of Spain and Florida. Maynard worked his signature and the date into the gold-embroidered bodice of

Tommy Thompson/Flagler College Archives

Terracotta medallions with Spanish proverbs stand above the entrances to the Hotel Ponce de Leon.

Discovery, one of the female images. Unlike frescoists, he painted on dry plaster, which began to deteriorate almost immediately in Florida's heat and humidity. Maintenance of the murals has been ongoing ever since.

Behind the painted plaster were wooden laths nailed to a complex web of wooden trusses that formed the dome. The same system supported the vault of the dining room. Also, buried inside the columns of the rotunda were tall, structural iron pipes supporting the central dome. Concrete was not the only innovative construction material used in the building.

From the rotunda, visitors going to the dining room ascended a flight of

Tommy Thompson/Flagler College Archives

The interior dome of the Hotel Ponce de Leon rises three stories.

Tommy Thompson/Flagler College Archives

A bronze statue of Elizabeth I of England greets visitors to the Hotel Ponce de Leon dining room.

Tommy Thompson/Flagler College Archives

The oak caryatids in the rotunda serve more than a decorative function. They surround iron structural pipes that support the mezzanine floor.

onyx and marble stairs that led to a low-ceilinged vestibule. To the left was the oak-paneled bar where gentlemen might pause to enjoy a before-dinner drink. The ladies turned right to the women's powder room, where they could socialize while awaiting their escorts. Then guests would be greeted at the dining room door by the maitre d', who would select and press one of the buttons on a wall panel to alert the party's assigned waiter that patrons would soon be arriving at their customary table in the expansive, vaulted dining room. To make this great room more intimate, Carrère and Hastings divided it into thirds with two rows of oak columns, a device they repeated in the rotunda and grand parlor. The east and west wings of the dining room were large, semicircular alcoves with walls of floor-to-ceiling windows. This, combined with the clerestory windows in the vault, flooded the room with light. Again, Maynard's murals crowded the walls and ceilings.

The windows were the creation of Louis C. Tiffany. In his late thirties at the time, Tiffany had just embarked on his

career in stained glass. The Ponce de Leon windows epitomize his early classical-style work. At the time, Tiffany considered himself an "interior decorator," but, unfortunately, we do not know

The huge dining room of the Hotel Ponce de Leon was divided into more intimate alcoves where guests dined amid opulence.

Flagler College Archives

Louis C. Tiffany founded Tiffany Glass Company to provide windows for the Hotel Ponce de Leon.

if his contributions to the hotel extended beyond the art glass panels. The Hotel Ponce de Leon's windows alone are sufficient tribute to his genius, and at the time they helped launch the public's enthusiasm for stained glass.

The furniture for the building came from the workshops of Pottier and Stymus of New York City and two other New York furniture makers. Pottier and Stymus were in the business of executing interior designs, including some they did for Flagler in later years. One of their senior craftsmen was the father of Bernard Maybeck, a friend of Thomas Hastings and junior associate in the firm of Carrère and Hastings. Later, the younger Maybeck became famous as a California

George W. Maynard employed Spanish motifs in his murals.

34

Tommy Thompson/Flagler College Archives

The semi-circular West Venido Room alcove of the dining room stands at the rear of the Hotel Ponce de Leon.

architect, and some historians have claimed to see Maybeck's hand in the interior decorations of the Hotel Ponce de Leon, but he is mentioned nowhere in the scant documentation relating to the hotel's construction. Hastings later claimed that he himself attempted "some" of the interior decorating "in the enthusiasm of youth." Thus it is impossible to establish with certainty the contributions to the interior decoration of the hotel made by Pottier and Stymus, Hastings, Tiffany, or Maybeck.

The rear of the dining room opened onto the kitchen, an important part of the large utility building standing at the back of the hotel complex. Here could be found the plumber's shop, electrician's room, carpenter's workshop, and, on the upper floors, living quarters for some of the staff. Behind this utility building stood the boiler room that provided steam heat for the guest rooms and powered the four Edison direct-current dynamos that generated the hotel's electricity.

Each of the hotel's 240 guest rooms had a fireplace as well as a radiator—but not a private bathroom. A communal bathroom down the hall was considered adequate at the time of the hotel's construction, but almost immediately public expectations rose, and the hotel began a long-term improvement program of installing semi-private baths between adjoining rooms.

In other ways, the Ponce was quite up to date from the beginning. There was a hydraulic elevator to whisk guests upstairs to their rooms. Close by the rotunda was a telegraph room, later updated to a telephone room. Guests could purchase newspapers from up North, sent in overnight by rail. There was a fully equipped barbershop. All of these amenities were located on one axis of the hotel in a long hall running from the central rotunda.

On the opposite axis, just off the rotunda, stood the final large public room of the hotel, the Grand Parlor. This room used a sophisticated palette of pastel blue, cream, and gold, in contrast to the more somber browns and gold of

A feminine ambiance pervades the Grand Parlor.

Tommy Thompson/Flagler College Archives

Crystal chandeliers in the Grand Parlor highlight the ceiling paintings of Virgillo Tojetti.

the rest of the interior. The windows generously admitted light, and overhead crystal chandeliers sparkled. In the room's four corners, the ceiling was covered with canvases painted by Virgillo Tojetti in his New York studio, then rolled up, shipped to St. Augustine, and pasted into place. These bright, cheerful paintings of plump cherubs sporting with doves and rabbits conveyed an optimistic, youthful sentiment.

On the parlor walls hung a collection of paintings by various artists. Most notable of these was a series of eight portraits by Joszi Arpad Koppay of Polish actress Helena Modjesha dressed for the roles of eight Shakespearean heroines. For a while, the monumental painting of Ponce de León in Florida by the celebrat-

Flagler College Archives

Tojetti's paintings were intended to convey a feeling of airy youthfulness.

The onyx mantle of the Grand Parlor.

Tommy Thompson/Flagler College Archives

ed landscape painter Thomas Moran also ornamented the parlor's walls. Moran had intended the painting for the United States House of Representatives, but after the House refused to purchase it, Flagler acquired it for his hotel. Flagler later removed it to his home in Palm Beach, and then the painting embarked on an obscure cross-country odyssey that ended with its purchase by Jacksonville's Cummer Museum of Art in 1996.

Flagler encouraged the fine arts in another interesting way. St. Augustine was already an artists' colony when Flagler came to town, and he capitalized on this situation by inviting some of the artists to take studios at the rear of the hotel. These seven lofts, with skylights facing north, became a social center during the winter season as hotel guests strolled Artists Row and purchased souvenir paintings to take home with them as remembrances of their Florida sojourns.

Best known of the Flagler studio artists was Martin Johnson Heade, the New England landscape painter and naturalist. Heade lived a quiet life in a cottage nearby, painting floral still lifes and gorgeous Florida sunsets. His most famous St. Augustine painting, *On the San Sebastian River*, depicts a boatman on the marshes of the San Sebastian, with an ominous thunderstorm moving in over the town and the towers of the

Hotel Ponce de Leon. Another artist, Frank Shapleigh, painted St. Augustine streetscapes during the winter, and in the summer he painted the White Mountains around Crawford Notch, New Hampshire. Other artists in residence over the years included Felix de Crano, W. Staples Drown, George W. Seavey (brother of the hotel manager), and Robert S. German.

The artists studios occupied a loft at the rear of the Hotel Ponce de Leon overlooking Memorial Presbyterian Church.

Flagler College Archives

New Hampshire Historical Society

Guests at the Hotel Ponce de Leon visited Frank Shapleigh's studio to purchase a memento of their stay.

THE CORDOVA
(CASA MONICA)

Just at the conclusion of the Hotel Ponce de Leon's first season, Flagler fell into ownership of a second hotel. Back in 1885, Franklin W. Smith, owner of Villa Zorayda, had bought a piece of property adjacent to Flagler's land and struck out on his own to build a luxury hotel. His erstwhile partner, Flagler, advised him against the project, but Smith went ahead anyway with a Moorish Revival structure he christened the Casa Monica. The still-uncompleted hotel opened a few days after the Ponce de Leon in January 1888, but with only three registered guests. Only a handful of patrons were willing to settle for what clearly amounted to second best. Most of the Casa Monica's two hundred rooms stood vacant. Four months later Smith sold the hotel to Flagler, who renamed it the Cordova Hotel.

Despite its dismal debut, Smith's creation had many virtues. The Cordova was constructed of a new, very dense mix of concrete, composed of Portland cement and sand dredged from the bay bottom. The hotel appeared to be one solid mass, but actually had been built as several separate units closely abutting each other. Its west wall featured an intricate tracery of concrete ornamentation, while wrought iron "kneeling balconies" extended from upper floor rooms. A large archway on the north façade, facing King Street, led into the main parlor where the color red predominated. To take advantage of Florida's sunny climate, Smith made the glass-roofed "Plaza del Sol" courtyard the showplace of the ground floor. While the layout of Carrère and Hastings' Ponce de Leon followed strictly symmetrical lines, the floor plan of Smith's Casa Monica wandered about, creating a warren of interesting interiors. No two rooms were alike.

Under Flagler's ownership, the Cordova enjoyed a few good years as a free-standing hotel in the early 1890s, but in mid-decade the red-trimmed parlor was converted into a series of storefronts and thereafter only the Cordova's upper-floor guest rooms were open for tenants. It never really turned a profit.

The west façade of the Hotel Cordova featured balconies made of either wood, iron, or concrete.

Tommy Thompson/Flagler College Archives

THE ALCAZAR

Flagler had long planned on a second hotel even before the Cordova fell into his lap. Early in the development of the Hotel Ponce de Leon, Flagler realized that his original vision of a grand resort hotel was too limited. One hotel could not stand alone. He would need another facility to house further amusements and to provide additional accommodations for guests. Thus, as soon as the Ponce de Leon was completed in May 1887 a second great hotel with an attached entertainment casino began to rise from the newly filled land just across King Street. Though it was grandly named the Alcazar (Caesar's House), Flagler envisioned it as a less expensive $2-a-day hotel. (Rooms at the Ponce started at $5

and went up to $100 for a few of the suites.)

Carrère and Hastings designed the Alcazar, and it was built by many of the same craftsmen who had just finished work on the Ponce de Leon. The more intimate size of the Alcazar allowed for close-up appreciation of the artistic ornamentation executed in terra cotta over the exterior. Its twin towers did not touch the sky, like those on the Ponce de Leon, and they served almost as a gate-

This architect's drawing of the Hotel Alcazar shows what the front portico would look like.

way to the snug courtyard, where the sound of spraying fountains conveyed a sense of serenity to all who walked its loggias.

In spite of the haste of the Alcazar's construction, the second hotel was not ready for guests in January 1888 when the Ponce de Leon opened. Wooden construction forms still encased the tops of its towers, and hotel employees, not millionaires, occupied its unfurnished rooms during that first season.

As it turned out, the Alcazar would never be finished as Carrère and Hastings planned it. The most obvious omission was the ellipse of shops which was intended to provide a decorative façade to the front of the hotel. The architects' drawing of the front elevation shows the ellipse in place, with red-tiled roof and ornamental terra cotta trim above formal Greek columns. The concrete foundations were poured (and are still in place), but for some reason the arcade was not built. Hastings would later express regret for this omission because it left the north face of the hotel with a stark, fortresslike appearance. Other small ornamentations of the hotel

were also deleted from Hastings' plans.

One can only speculate why these shortcuts were taken. We do know that during the summer of 1888 Florida was swept by a yellow fever epidemic. St. Augustine escaped the disease only by imposing a strict quarantine on communication with the outside world. This slowed work on the Alcazar and may have led to the elimination of portions of the building not deemed essential. A few years after the opening of the hotel, vines began to climb and cover the outside of the building, somewhat softening the appearance of the massive concrete walls.

In the wake of the yellow fever epidemic, the official opening of the Hotel Alcazar became a small affair. On Christmas day, 1888, the first guests registered and then, together with some invited townsfolk, shared a dinner in the "beautifully frescoed and brilliantly lighted" café with manager Seavey as host. After dinner the party took a tour of the Alcazar's central atrium with its reflecting pool and surrounding arcade of shops. Then they proceeded to the Casino and Baths areas behind the

Alcazar to inspect the work which was nearing completion.

In the section of the complex known as the Baths, which Carrère and Hastings had situated just behind the hotel, large slabs of marble were being hoisted into place for the walls and floors of the Turkish and Russian baths. The Turkish bath was a room of dry heat where the temperature was set at 160-180 degrees Fahrenheit. In the Russian bath, a steam room soon to be known as the "Senate," patrons sat on marble tiers wrapped in "togas" to endure the 112-120 degree heat. Flagler hired a Turkish attendant from Chicago's Palmer House to supervise the baths.

Advertising for the baths touted them as cure-alls for heart disease, as well as for "gout, rheumatism, liver and kidney diseases, neurosthenia and obesity." The logic of treatment, to the extent that the treatment was explained, seems to have focused upon relieving "congestion" in affected internal organs by drawing the patient's blood away from the body core to the skin through induced sweating. A patron would enter the Baths from the hotel or the Casino and go to one of forty cubicle dressing rooms to disrobe. Then he would follow a regimen prescribed by his physician or by the staff, which might involve being sprayed from a hose and being

Alcazar

Steam Room

Gymnasium

45

Tennis courts covered the grounds at the rear of the Casino.

Artesian well water entered the Casino pool from below, while sunshine entered from a skylight above.

given a shampoo, followed by a steam in the Russian bath, then a stint in the circular shower bath, where a variety of jets of water would be sprayed on the patient—then back to the steam room, and, finally, a quick dip in the cold plunge. Afterward he might repair to the "resting room" for an aromatic oil rubdown and a glass of Clarendon Springs mineral water.

Also in the Baths was a small but elegantly furnished gymnasium where patrons could exercise amid Carrère and Hastings' version of classical Greek architecture. There were dumbbells, pulleys, free weights, Indian clubs, punching bags, parallel and horizontal bars, and oriental rugs onto which exercisers dripped their sweat.

Women might use the Baths and gymnasium at scheduled times, usually the morning hours in most seasons, when female attendants supervised the treatments.

To the rear of the Baths stood the Casino building, a massive square structure which could be entered from the two arched porticoes connecting it with the back of the Alcazar, or one could gain entry by climbing the broad stairways at the rear of the building. If the exterior appearance of the Casino tended to be overpowering, the interior was elegant. Carrère and Hastings had used eight soaring gray concrete arches rising three stories from the bottom of the swimming pool floor to circumscribe the rectangular pool area. The rest of the interior was painted ivory white. Light flooded in from the glassed-over roof above the pool and reflected back from the translucent green water onto the walls, creating a pleasant, mysterious effect. In the evenings one thousand electric lights illuminated the interior. On the first floor an arcade ran around the pool, and here were located the dressing rooms. One story above, completely encircling the pool area, was the ballroom with its highly polished wood floor. A stage at one end of the ballroom could be used for plays, lectures, and musical performances.

The water in the pool came from an artesian well sunk 1,400 feet deep into the Florida aquifer. At that depth the water maintained a natural temperature of eighty degrees, so it was unnecessary to heat the pool to keep it at a comfortable temperature for swimming. The only drawback was that the water, like that used in the plumbing of the hotels, contained dissolved sulfur, and even aerating it did not completely remove the "rotten-egg" smell. The water in the pool constantly circulated, entering through a small cascade at one side of the pool and draining from below. The shallow west end of the pool was three and a half feet deep and sloped down to six and a half feet at the east end. Connected with the main pool were two semicircular pools at the east and west ends. The eastern pool was for the men and the western pool for the women. A partition separated the pool at the women's end so that those too modest to swim in public could take a dip in private.

The Casino did not open to the public until February 22, 1889, Washington's

Changing rooms surround the private women's pool.

Flagler College Archives

47

Birthday, traditionally the day for the grandest ball of the season. For the two previous days St. Augustine's tourists had been confined to their hotels—playing progressive euchre, that year's popular card game—by the pouring rain and winds of a northeaster. On opening night guests making their way to the Casino through the sodden streets were welcomed by a large sign between the towers of the hotel which spelled "ALCAZAR" in colored electric lights. Inside, the Ponce de Leon's orchestra and the Alcazar band played from opposite sides of the mezzanine ballroom above the pool. The Casino was filled with the curious who turned out to enjoy themselves and see what additional novelty Flagler had wrought.

In the weeks afterward, the Casino became one of the Flagler hotel complex's most popular gathering places. For twenty-five cents anyone from town or the other hotels could enter the Casino. Rental bathing suits were available, as were male and female swim-

The Alcazar and Ponce de Leon face each other across a park.

Tommy Thompson/Flagler College Archives

ming instructors for those wishing to learn to swim. It quickly became fashionable for bathers to use the pool about noon, when the hotel band would present the first of its two daytime concerts in the Casino. Those who did not swim could sit at tables around the pool and watch or tend to their knitting and newspapers while they enjoyed the music. In the evenings weekly "pool entertainments" took place, which included daring high dives from the ballroom balcony into the pool, swings from the gymnasium apparatus hanging from the rafters, games of water polo played by teams from various groups in the city, swimming races, and an assortment of comic events such as tub races. After the entertainment the pool would be open for general swimming, and the evening would top off with dancing and refreshments in the ballroom.

Some of the edge was taken off the excitement of the Alcazar's premier season and the second year of the Ponce de Leon as the preceding summer's yellow fever epidemic had frightened many Northerners out of coming to Florida. The cause of "Yellow Jack" was unknown at the time, and no one had

Guests entering the Hotel Ponce de Leon walked through the courtyard, past the fountain and under a terracotta archway.

found a cure, so the overly cautious refused to trust the folk wisdom that the fever never occurred after the first heavy frost of the winter. A count of the town's hotel registers had totaled 50,000 guests in the 1888 season, but only 29,000 registered in 1889. It was an "off year" for tourism.

Nevertheless, Flagler had planned a grand affair for March 1889 to publicize the Alcazar and Casino. It was the Alicia Hospital Fair and Ball, and it turned out to be the highlight of the season. The event was promoted as the most extravagant charity affair of its kind ever given in the South. Five thousand dollars were spent on fireworks alone. Festivities were spread over the three days of March 12, 13, and 14. Proceeds went to support Alicia Hospital, the new community hospital, which the second Mrs. Flagler sponsored as her personal contribution to the town.

On the first night of the fair twelve hundred people jammed into the Casino to play games at the various booths and to purchase items made for or donated to the fair. Bright Japanese lanterns swayed from the rafters, while in the pool a colorfully decorated Venetian gondola floated, from which the Alcazar band played popular tunes. Mrs. Flagler presided over a booth featuring a mechanical racetrack where wagers could be placed on toy horses at twenty-five cents a try. On the third day of the fair, festivities extended across King Street to the Ponce de Leon for a formal ball. Guests could go from one venue to another, but they were obliged to run a gauntlet of rain showers that forced cut-off of the outside electric light decorations. Despite the refusal of nature to cooperate, the fair was a spectacular success and would be held annually for

several years thereafter.

A week following the fair, ex-President Grover Cleveland paid a return visit to St. Augustine. As in the previous year, Cleveland toured the town in a carriage, held a public reception, and stayed in a suite in the Ponce de Leon, but this time he paid several visits to the newly opened Alcazar and Casino. Flagler escorted Cleveland's party to the Casino, where former Secretary of State Thomas Bayard donned a rented swimsuit and jumped into the pool. After dinner Cleveland's entourage returned to the Casino to watch a high-diving exhibition.

The second season of Flagler's hotel venture concluded at the end of the month of March, but Flagler decided to keep the Alcazar open through the summer to see if it could make a profit as a summer resort. Those guests remaining when the Ponce de Leon closed moved their baggage over to the Alcazar, and six musicians from the Ponce orchestra remained behind when the rest of their group departed for work in Northern resorts. Flagler hoped that

Flagler College Archives

Parlor of the Hotel Alcazar.

Southerners from the interior regions would come to St. Augustine during the sultry summer months to enjoy the sea breezes. However, this did not prove to be the case. Flagler would try again the next year in 1890, but then wrote off the experiment as a failure.

Nevertheless, the Alcazar had turned out to be more popular as a hotel than Flagler had anticipated. The original intent was that the Alzacar and Casino be primarily a complex of shops and amusements for guests of the Ponce de Leon, with rooms only as an ancillary service for the larger hotel. However, Flagler immediately perceived that the Alcazar would be able to stand on its own as a full-fledged hotel. This required changes in the building to make it, in Flagler's words, "every bit as good" as the Ponce de Leon.

The first requirement was for a larger dining room to expand the small café, since the hotel would need to pro-

The courtyard of the Hotel Alcazar before the addition of the fourth floor.

The Alcazar with its fourth floor addition.

vide guests with three meals a day, not just breakfast. The café occupied the first floor on the south side of the hotel quadrangle. Just outside in back of the hotel were two small patios between the hotel and the Baths section. These were covered by iron-framed glass enclosures and became extensions of the dining room. Later, in 1897, the café was expanded on its opposite side by taking in the south loggia of the hotel's central courtyard. This was done by enclosing the spaces under the arches with wooden and glass partitions. Finally, in 1902 a large concrete-walled dining room was built onto the rear of the Alcazar at its southeast corner. In order to build this addition a section of the east portico between the hotel and the Casino had to be demolished, as well as the small glassed-in patio room on that side.

In the summer of 1891 major changes were made to other parts of the Alcazar. Forty new rooms were added to the original seventy-five rooms by constructing a fourth floor around the rear three sides of the hotel quadrangle. To do this, windows were cut into the roof parapet, a new peaked roof was added above the added story, and a decorative

In Flagler's day there was a boat basin at the foot of the Plaza. The Confederate Monument, Public Market, and Catholic Church still stand on the Plaza.

Flagler College Archives

balustrade of brick was added around the top of the exterior walls to hide the new roof. The original parlor on the second floor became bedrooms, and a row of four shops on the west side of the first floor were consolidated to form one large parlor. The roof of the portico connecting the hotel to the Casino on the west side was enclosed so guests could pass from the second floor of the Alcazar to the Casino without going out of doors. Lastly, the builders began a lengthy program of adding semi-private baths between rooms to replace the two communal bathrooms on each of the upper floors.

Heating remained primitive in the Alcazar. Public areas of the building were heated by steam radiators, but many of the rooms were furnished only with small iron stoves for use during cold snaps.

Over the years the Alcazar would develop its own clientele—people who returned year after year to spend the season. One reason for the popularity of the Alcazar was its less stuffy atmosphere compared to the high-toned Ponce de Leon, where formal dress was required at evening meals. The Alcazar had a cozy homelike feel. A local society magazine noted: "The people of St. Augustine are proud of the Ponce de Leon, but they love the Alcazar." In most seasons the Alcazar actually hosted more guests than the larger Ponce de Leon. This was because it opened earlier and closed later, making its season two months longer than the Ponce's.

In 1893 disaster struck the Casino. On the night of January 24 a night watchman patrolling the building detected a light inside a hotel employee's room on the fourth floor above the Casino ballroom. The worker was awakened and a small fire was discovered in the ceiling around the electric light fixture. Workers attempted to extinguish the flame, but the ceiling collapsed, revealing a much larger fire in the wooden roof trusses above. By then local firefighters had arrived and began battling the fire, but the stream of water from their hoses did not effectively reach the fourth floor. St. Augustine's mayor telegraphed Jacksonville for help, and a fire engine was sent to the scene on a railroad flatcar. For a while the fire threatened to enter the Baths area, and the battle was centered at this point. By dawn the worst had passed, and the Alcazar staff handed out coffee and sandwiches to the firefighters. The interiors of the top two stories of the Casino were reduced to ashes, but the building's cement construction had averted complete destruction. During the summer and fall, repairs were completed, including a new electrical system with wires enclosed in brass conduits.

The rewiring was part of ongoing efforts to upgrade the utilities of the hotel. The Alcazar had originally received its electric power from the Ponce de Leon's generators, but in 1891 two Edison direct-current dynamos were installed in the boiler room building at the rear of the Alcazar so it could generate its own power. In 1892 all Flagler's hotels began using soft water piped in from his own waterworks located several miles outside town. This ended the days of describing sulfur water to guests as really "mineral water" that was good for you.

The dynamo room of the Hotel Alcazar.

Flagler College Archives

The Flagler family mausoleum stands in the foreground of Memorial Presbyterian Church.

THE RISES AND DECLINES OF ST. AUGUSTINE AS PREMIER RESORT TOWN

The opening of the 1890 season marked the beginning of St. Augustine's years of eminence as the Winter Newport of America. Flagler's three elegant hotels formed the heart of a genteel resort society for the country's foremost families. Flagler's investments in imagination and money began to pay generous dividends. The benefits radiated out into the St. Augustine community to provide the old town with the amenities of modern times.

Flagler's work crews continued to add to the network of streets around the hotels that were paved with asphalt. Flagler built a new railroad depot and a new city hall. Grace Methodist Church, another Carrère and Hastings Spanish Renaissance creation, rose just north of the Ponce de Leon. Flagler erected the church in exchange for the land where the Methodists' Olivet Church once stood—now part of the front garden of the Alcazar. Flagler's other church was a labor of love that grew out of personal tragedy. Early in 1889 his daughter Jennie Louise Benedict died following childbirth. In her honor Flagler dedicated Memorial Presbyterian Church. Carrère and Hastings again designed the building, but this time they chose Italian Renaissance as the style. The church echoed the spirit of St. Marks in Venice, and its blond terra cotta ornamentation and copper dome set it off from the gray walls and orange roof tiles of the hotels across the way.

Other blows fell on Henry Flagler's personal life in the 1890s. He had built a classic colonial style home called Kirkside for his wife just to the west of Memorial Presbyterian. But tragedy cut short the life the couple anticipated in their new home. Vivacious Alicia Flagler loved extravagant gowns and jewelry and the

Flagler College Archives

Grace Methodist Church

Flagler College Archives

Memorial Presbyterian Church

social whirl of resort life, in which her husband participated only reluctantly. In the midst of all this lively activity, she began to act erratically. Gradually she descended into a world of delirium. Flagler called upon several doctors for treatment, but her mental problems were beyond the reach of that day's science. Among other things, she fantasized that she was engaged to the tsar of Russia. Finally, an exhausted Flagler placed her in an asylum in New York state where she would live in physical comfort financed by a multi-million-dollar trust fund. Her mental derangement continued until her death in 1930.

While Flagler underwent his trials with his wife, he and his only surviving offspring, Henry "Harry" Harkness Flagler, grew farther and farther apart. Young Harry dropped out of college, and Flagler brought him to St. Augustine to learn the

A walk down Hospital Street would take tourists through the oldest part of the Ancient City. Artist Frank Shapleigh made this painting as a souvenir.

hotel and railroad business, but the son's spirit did not suit the harsh world of business enterprise. Harry returned to New York. "Harry's desertion of me has made my burden much heavier," lamented Flagler, "and I constantly wonder why this additional sorrow was necessary." Harry would not see his father again until Flagler was on his deathbed.

Living in New York City, Harry Flagler immersed himself in the cultural milieu of artistic society. He married into the wealthy Lamont family and became a patron of both the Symphony Society and Philharmonic-Symphony Society of New York. He would die in 1952, a well-remembered member of New York's musical world.

In the days before the automobile gave them mobility, winter visitors to Florida tended to remain in one location for weeks and even months at a time. Thus resorts had to find a variety of amusements to keep their patrons occupied. The antique town of St. Augustine had several natural advantages for this type of recreation. Winter visitors inevitably explored the town to see its well-known curiosities: the Oldest House,

on St. Francis Street; the "dungeons" of old Fort Marion; the Fountain of Youth; and the Alligator Farm, on Anastasia Island. Some went in for yachting, fishing, and—for the adventurous—swimming in the surf of the Atlantic.

Tennis blossomed into one of the most popular sports of the day. Just north of the Ponce de Leon and also immediately south of the Casino, Flagler constructed asphalt courts on which the game could be played. To publicize the sport and his new resort, Flagler sponsored the Tropical Tennis Tournament in 1888 and in following years. Some of the top-ranked players in the nation contested for the trophy, a huge sterling silver replica of the City Gate. During the tournaments crowds of onlookers watched from bleachers while the hotel bands played nearby. Regular guests of the hotels used the courts on a daily basis, and there were tennis instructors on staff to teach the game to novices.

In the middle and late 1890s bicycling became the rage. During the '97 season the tennis courts behind the Casino were even temporarily turned into a "bicycle academy" to meet the

The Tropical Tennis Tournament attracted some of the best players in the nation. The Hotel Ponce de Leon artists studios can be seen in the background.

A "bicycle academy" occupied the Casino tennis courts one season.

public demand for instruction in riding a "wheel." The town council was obliged to pass traffic ordinances to handle the new mechanical traffic on the streets, and main roads received a layer of oyster shell since bike wheels could not cope with Florida's natural deep white sand. The local social magazine *The Tatler*, which had a lady editor, commented favorably on the liberating effect "wheeling" had on women's fashions.

The other great sporting fad of the decade was golf. The green surrounding Fort Marion even became a course—with the moat presenting a formidable water trap. At the shops in the Alcazar one could purchase balls and other golf accessories, and—as Flagler's promotional brochures pointed

The tides rose and fell around the Tower Tee of Flagler's golf course.

Flagler College Archives

out—the East Coast Golf Club was just five minutes from the hotels "by wheel or coach." A carriage to the links departed from the hotels every half hour. Flagler's nine-hole golf course was situated at the extreme south end of the peninsula on which the town of St. Augustine rests. The land was virtually a salt marsh, and the fourth tee stood atop a stone tower built on land over which the tides ebbed and flowed. Flagler's brochure attempted to put the best possible light on the scene: "A short velvety turf covers almost the entire course; the teeing grounds are made of hard muck, and the putting greens, of the regulation size, are built of the same material, well tamped, and sprinkled daily with a layer of sharp beach sand." A few years later the Flagler system would build the much more impressive Ponce de Leon Golf Club about five miles north of his hotels.

Bowling was also available in the Casino, and it seems to have enjoyed a steady popularity despite the inconvenient location of the lanes. In order to get to the bowling alley, guests were required to leave the Casino and reenter from the rear of the building beneath the large stairways. Here, in a dim, dank hall beside the concrete bulkhead of the swimming pool, eight lanes could be found. Nevertheless, bowling had its devotees, even among the ladies.

Shopping has customarily been part of the tourist experience. St. George Street was lined with little shops, but Flagler's hotels also housed a variety of specialty stores. On the first floor of the Cordova visitors could stroll

Ward Foster's book store occupied the corner shop in the Hotel Cordova.

Flagler College Archives

through "El Unico" in search of tobacco products and curiosities, or visit Ward Foster's shop to find a book to pass the time. Foster gained such a reputation as an authority on railroad, steamship, and hotel accommodations that he started his own travel agency, Ask Mister Foster, which expanded into an international chain of agencies.

Although the original concept of the Alcazar as a "cosmopolitan bazaar" had been scaled back, it did contain a variety of shops. The most noted of these was Greenleaf and Crosby Jewelers, which occupied the room on the left of the entrance to the Alcazar's courtyard. Among their most popular items were souvenir spoons with impressions of the City Gate, alligators, the Hotel Ponce de Leon, or Spain's coat of arms. Marshall Williams' shop sold tropical fruit jellies packaged in boxes embossed with the Alcazar's picture. Madame Schutz's sold tortoise shell goods, as well as hair ornaments. She also curled hair. Fuller's Japanese Palace featured Oriental products, including hara-kiri knives claimed to be stained with real blood. White, Howard and Company sold clothing: imported gowns, carriage and yachting wear, "tennis costumes," hats, etc.

If hotel guests were the first estate of resort society, the hotel employees formed a second estate—fully as numerous as the first. They lived in a sphere overlapping that of the guests, but strictly and distinctly separate. A hotel system within the hotel system existed to care for the employees. White male workers lived upstairs in the Casino and in the utility wing of the Ponce de Leon. Here also were several dining rooms for the various grades of hotel employees. Women lived in the laundry building near the railroad depot on Valencia Street. The "colored barracks" on South Cordova Street housed black men. Most of the hotel employees were career workers who migrated from Northern to Southern resorts following the seasons. Local residents of town were considered unreliable workers because they were likely to take off if the mullet were running on the beach.

A variety of skilled individuals were employed by the Flagler hotels: French chefs, musicians, engineers, plumbers, carpenters, gardeners, dynamo-tenders, and two unobtrusive Pinkerton detectives to watch out for the bunko artists who followed wealthy travelers. One electrician's assistant had the job of circulating to find and replace light bulbs as they burned out. Another tended the hotels' herd of eleven milk cows. Flagler and his managers paid the men in key positions so well that many remained with the system for years.

Hotel employment counted as very good work for black men and women, with dining room waiters holding the most prestigious jobs. The Ponce de Leon and Alcazar waiters bore the added responsibility of fielding baseball teams to play spirited and entertaining games for the guests. Hotel manager Seavey was a huge baseball fan, and he had induced Flagler to have Albert G. Spalding design a ball field. White professional teams sometimes played winter exhibition games there.

Ponce de Leon headwaiter Frank Thompson captained the hotel's team, which included several players from the Cuban Giants of the Negro Professional League. Thompson also chaired the hotel

workers' "progressive association" that dealt with problems among St. Augustine's black resort employee population.

Cake walks were a standard feature of resort life during this time, sponsored either by the hotels or by the black employees of the hotels to raise money for their charities. Although the cake walks pandered to racial stereotypes, they were one of the few occasions when white folks and black folks could gather together on a socially amicable basis in an age when the color line was strictly drawn. There was an accepted order to the proceedings. First a chorus or quartet would sing plantation songs, followed by "buck and

The winners of a cake walk.

wing" dancing by the men, and then the cake walk itself. Black couples, dressed in their Sunday best, women in large-brimmed hats and men with fancy walking sticks, would parade before a panel of judges while a band played in accompaniment. Couples would be judged on bearing, carriage, and stylishness in making turns. One by one the couples would be eliminated until only one couple remained to "take the cake." The judges were themselves judged by the audience to see if their opinions agreed with the general consensus. Noted guests, such as comedian Joseph Jefferson and Admiral George Dewey, were often made judges. Following the cake walk, the white guests would take the floor to dance the evening away.

In 1898 the editor of *The Tatler* attended a presentation on the stage of the Casino and was dumbfounded at what she saw: "The reproduction of living, moving men and women, life size, of galloping horses, dashing trains, gave very general satisfaction. . . . While the audience was a good one, had the people of St. Augustine had the least idea of what the show would be, the great hall

would have been crowded." The amazed editor was evidently ignorant of the term "moving picture" and had no word to label what she had seen.

Innovation was the hallmark of the era, and change was bringing St. Augustine's newly won standing as the epitome of winter resorts to an end after only a brief half-dozen seasons. Annual house counts in Flagler's hotels began declining. The explanation was easy to discern. Florida's frontier was rapidly moving southward with the construction

The campanile of the Catholic Church rises behind a tower of the Hotel Ponce de Leon. Beyond that stretches Matanzas Bay and the salt flats of Anastasia Island.

of each mile of railroad track. Pioneer tourists discovered that the more southerly reaches of the peninsula offered the guarantee of warm weather all the time, while St. Augustine suffered from occasional cold snaps. In 1895 St. Augustine experienced the great freeze of the century. Oranges froze solid on the branches, and all the exotic shrubbery around the Ponce de Leon blackened and died. Florida's west coast developer, Henry B. Plant, had already opened his version of an exotic pleasure palace, the Tampa Bay Hotel, on the Gulf Coast in 1891. The story is that Plant invited Flagler to the grand opening, and Flagler asked, "Where the heck is Tampa?" Plant supposedly replied, "Just follow the crowds."

Henry Flagler was quick to perceive what must be done, and his Florida vision expanded. He extended his Florida East Coast Railway southward. First to Ormond Beach, where he bought and enlarged a hotel, and then to Palm Beach, where he purchased a whole island and began to build his own city. In 1894 the Royal Poinciana Hotel, reputed to be the largest wooden building in the world, opened its doors and welcomed the elite patrons who had formerly graced the elegant rooms of the Hotel Ponce de Leon. Nearby, on the Atlantic shore, Flagler built the Breakers, another palatial hotel. Palm Beach would become the Winter Newport. Below Palm Beach, Miami beckoned, and, beyond that, Key West.

The great financial panic of the 1893 also devastated St. Augustine's fortunes. Hard times hit America in the 1890s, and the economic depression hit the wealthy as well as the working class. *The Tatler* editorially moaned, "While there are very few persons who are not experiencing 'a shrinkage in dividends,' or a reduction in salaries, there are very many who have adopted habits of economy not absolutely necessary." Such pleas for more liberal spending fell on deaf ears. The Alcazar almost didn't open in 1894, and when it did in February, it opened only for rooms, requiring guests to take their meals at the Ponce de Leon or the Cordova. The Casino was in operation, but entertainments were cut back to save expenses. The following season the Alcazar again delayed its opening until February, but a semblance of prosperity was returning.

By the time William McKinley was inaugurated in 1897 and the nation resumed its way toward good times again, the mantle of Winter Newport had clearly passed to Flagler's Palm Beach. Henceforth, Flagler would devote his energies to building his railroad southward, eventually all the way down the Florida Keys to Key West. St. Augustine became a way station to south Florida. The season in St. Augustine now took on a definite directional pattern. In December and January guests stayed a few days on their way south, and in March and April they stayed a few days on their way north. Only the old regulars stayed the winter in St. Augustine, and they tended to be just that—old. St. Augustine's ancient habits of being slow and decadent came to the fore again.

One thing endured: the monumental buildings Flagler had built. Never again would he build anything as solid, tasteful, or important as he did in his first venture in Florida.

To some degree Flagler had

By the early twentieth century, ladies in the Ponce de Leon courtyard were wearing more casual dresses and hemlines were rising just a little.

"soured" on St. Augustine early on because of bickering with the city government over things like streets and utilities, and because of the local populace's resistance to his leadership. For example, Flagler opposed laying a prosaic streetcar line down King Street between his ornate hotels. The city council went ahead anyway. Many old timers in St. Augustine blamed Flagler for rising taxes and the various headaches associated with rapid population growth. In a 1906 letter Flagler expressed his disgust with the community: "I have realized from the begin-

Henry Flagler with his third wife Mary Lily.

ning that St. Augustine was a dull place, but it does seem as though twenty years would stir up some little measure of public spirit; enough to keep the only street we have to the Railroad in decent condition."

During the 1890s Flagler made Palm Beach his winter home. From here he directed his ongoing railroad and hotel enterprises in South Florida. In 1901 he arranged for the Florida legislature to pass a law making insanity grounds for divorce and ended his marriage to the now-institutionalized Alicia. He soon married for a third time. The bride, Mary Lily Kenan, came from a respected North Carolina family. He was seventy-one and she was thirty-four. As a wedding gift Flagler had the old team of Carrère and Hastings, McGuire and McDonald, and Pottier and Stymus build a magnifi-

Flagler's home Whitehall in Palm Beach is today the Henry Morrison Flagler Museum.

cent marble palace, which he named "Whitehall," next door to Flagler's sprawling Royal Poinciana Hotel. Some in Palm Beach society gossiped about the Flaglers' May-November marriage, but Henry and Mary Lily seemed to enjoy life together, although she, like his second wife, thrived on the social scene, while Henry thought parties a waste of time and could not tolerate small-talk. Sometimes guests entering Whitehall found Flagler napping on a sofa in the grand columned entrance hall with a handkerchief over his eyes.

Within a few years Flagler launched his most ambitious and expensive project to date: extending his railroad over the open water and string of islands that made up the Florida Keys. Flagler justified the expense by saying Key West would become the closest deep-water port to the soon-to-be-completed Panama Canal. Some of those who knew Flagler, however, thought he undertook the monumental project just to create another challenge for himself. The enterprise would absorb most of his attention for the next six years.

Yet even as Flagler seemed most absorbed with southernmost Florida, he began, after a decade's absence, to spend more time in St. Augustine. He

The Flagler hotel empire grew to extend from Jacksonville Beach to Key West and Nassau. The Hotel Ponce de Leon's crest is at the center of this array, symbolizing its preeminence.

and Mary Lily would arrive in mid-December and remain for a few weeks before moving on to Palm Beach. They held receptions and presided over an annual Christmas party for children of friends around a giant Christmas tree in the rotunda of the Ponce de Leon. St. Augustinians who feared Flagler had abandoned their town were pleased to see their patron return.

Even the tourists started to return with the beginning of a new century, and winter house counts at local hotels exceeded all previous records. Some local hotels even set up cots in their hallways. However, most of the newcomers were a new kind of tourist, "people of moderate means" as a promotional brochure put it. One of Flagler's lieutenants noted with disdain that most of the guests in town were "cheap people," who would never give the first thought to staying in a place like the Ponce de Leon, which by then had begun to look like a faded dowager from a bygone epoch. Public tastes were turning toward a less formal lifestyle. A Spanish Renaissance palace was not the appropriate setting for a band to play

new songs like "If You Love Your Baby, Make the Goo Goo Eyes."

To accommodate the increased numbers of people desiring rooms, Flagler decided to refurbish the Cordova Hotel, which had never been a success, and to make it a part of the Alcazar. This was accomplished by building a bridge across Cordova Street between the second stories of the two buildings. The work was completed in time for the 1903 season. The local newspaper reported that guests regis-

Early in the twentieth century the Alcazar and Cordova hotels were connected by a bridge over Cordova Street.

tering at the Alcazar would scarcely realize they had crossed the bridge into another building. The Cordova lost its independent identity, becoming known as just the "Alcazar Annex."

As the modern era progressed, Henry Flagler himself looked more and more like a relic from a bygone era. In 1912 he rode the first ceremonial train into Key West to mark the completion of the Overseas Extension. A brass band and lines of U.S. sailors were there to greet him. School children sang his praises, but the old man whispered, "I can hear the children, but I cannot see them." His eyes, ears, and body were failing, but not his mind or iron will. When he planned a visit to the Ponce de Leon, he wrote ahead to get the width of the gate in the hotel's portcullis—to make sure his wheelchair could pass through.

Early in 1913, Flagler fell down a stairway in Whitehall, breaking his hip. Confined to bed, his condition soon deteriorated. His friend Dr. Anderson hurried to Palm Beach, but reported home: "Mr. Flagler still lingers. He may do so for some time longer but no one has any hope he will recover. . . . He has always dreaded going—but now he does not know it, for his mind wanders. Most of the time he thinks he is in a railroad car." Officers in Flagler's East Coast Railway empire sent out coded telegrams to keep company official apprised of developments.

Flagler previously had let it be known that when he died, he would like to be interred alongside his first wife, Mary, and daughter, Jennie Louise, in the Memorial Presbyterian Church. On May 20, 1913, Flagler died. His mortal remains were brought to St. Augustine by a black-draped train and rested

Flagler's funeral leaves the front gate of the Hotel Ponce de Leon.

under the dome of the Hotel Ponce de Leon while the citizenry filed past to pay their last respects. Florida would not see his likes again.

The next several years were good ones for the St. Augustine hotels, despite the problems arising from World War I. When war broke out in Europe in 1914, Florida's hotel managers feared that tourists would stay home and conserve their money. James McGuire, who had settled down in St. Augustine to look after Flagler's buildings, wrote Northern resort managers to find out how the war had affected their business. "Prospects for a successful season do not look bright," he concluded. But, to his surprise, it turned out that more visitors than usual came because they were unable to travel to Europe.

Then when the United States entered the war in 1917, there was concern that government control of the railroads would discourage tourist travel. This proved to be true, but only for the 1918 season. Plans were made for the Alcazar to remain closed in 1919, but with the end of the war the demand for rooms led to its reopening. One significant change did alter life among the hundreds of employees working at the hotels. Government worries about a manpower shortage for the draft led to an order that the hotel managers replace black waiters, who had been a traditional part of the hotel staff, with white waitresses.

The Roaring Twenties witnessed a decade of unprecedented prosperity for St. Augustine. Thomas Hastings stopped by, as he said, "like Rip Van Winkle," to see the progress the town had made since 1888. In the intervening years he and Carrère (who died in a traffic accident in 1911) had built the Jefferson Hotel in Richmond, the New York Public Library, the U.S. Senate Office Building, and numerous other public buildings and private residences in the United States and abroad. Hastings walked around the Hotel Ponce de Leon and commented that it had stood the test of time well. He observed that if he had it to do over he would alter the exterior a little and change some of the interiors. "The dining room, however," he declared, "I think I would leave as it is."

By the 1920s the presidency of the Florida East Coast Hotel Company had passed to William R. Kenan, Flagler's brother-in-law, who began extensive renovations to modernize the Ponce de Leon and Alcazar. Things were looking up as increased house counts led to higher profits.

Old John D. Rockefeller and his sons paid a visit. A jazz band regularly held forth in the afternoons for tea in the palm garden on the Ponce west lawn. Daredevil pilot Doug Davis piloted his biplane between the twin towers of the hotel. A stock ticker machine rattled away in an office off the rotunda. Mack Sennett's bathing beauties strutted the stage of the Jefferson Theater. Will Rogers waxed philosophical about current events in the Casino ballroom. Young people danced in the street between the Alcazar and Cordova. In 1925 and 1926 the AAU Women's National Swimming Championships were held in the Casino pool, with Gertrude Ederle as the star performer. Parked automobiles lined the old carriage path behind the hotel. Boom-time Florida sizzled.

But those automobiles symbolized the demise of the traditional grand resort hotel. More and more winter visitors drove right past the Ponce de Leon on U.S. 1, the "Sunshine Highway," headed for younger, more lively cities like Ft. Lauderdale and Miami. These tourists sought the convenience of low-cost motor courts to spend the night and spurned the elaborate amenities of Flagler's hotels. The respected novelist William Dean Howells, a winter resident of town, observed: "People now do not want that series of drawing and dining-rooms which open from the inner patio of the Ponce de Leon; and if they did, they would not have the form fitly to inhabit them; their short skirts and their lounge-coats are not for such gracious interiors, but rather for the golf-links."

Beginning in 1924, while the boom was yet in full swing, the Ponce de Leon and Alcazar began to run annual deficits and never reported a profit thereafter. The bursting of the Florida land boom in 1926 and the beginning of the Great Depression following the stock market crash of 1929 spelled the doom of the Royal Poinciana in Palm

Beach and Flagler's Royal Palm in Miami. Hotel company president Kenan tried to adjust by turning the Cordova into a low-cost hotel in 1927. After 1932 both the Cordova and Alcazar were closed, and the Ponce de Leon remained in operation only for sentimental reasons. William R. Kenan vowed that as long as he lived, the Ponce would carry on.

By 1932 the Ponce de Leon was averaging just forty-one paying guests per day. Staff had been reduced to a skeleton crew, working at half-salary. Still, the old hotel remained a great source of civic pride for local citizens. The great dining room of the hotel was St. Augustinians' favorite place to ring in each new year. There were also charity balls, tea parties, and club dinners. When World War II broke out, relief organizations held dances in the dining room to raise money for aid to Great Britain.

The attack on Pearl Harbor that launched the United States into the war struck Florida like a thunderbolt. It came just at the beginning of the winter tourist season that meant life or death for the economy of many Florida com-

munities. Travel restrictions, nighttime blackouts, and gas rationing seemed to signal continued hard times for the hotel trade. Florida's business leaders and politicians petitioned Washington to come to the rescue. The government responded by leasing resort hotels all over the state for use as military bases and training facilities. The Hotel Ponce de Leon was taken over by the Coast Guard as a center for basic training. By the fall of 1942 more than two thousand Coast Guard cadets were living in the hotel. The tramping of young men's feet down the hallways brought great sheets of plaster down from the ceilings. The old building came to life with a vengeance.

Black Coast Guard trainees lived in

Flagler College Archives

The Hotel Ponce de Leon became a Coast Guard training center during World War II.

segregated quarters upstairs under the rafters of the utility wing of the Ponce. Among them was the young artist Jacob Lawrence, who had already been featured in a New York City showing of his "Migration Series" paintings chronicling the black exodus from the South to the North.

During the war the furnishings of the Ponce went across the street to the Alcazar, where they were treated with preservatives and wrapped for storage. A reporter for the *St. Augustine Record* walked through the halls, packed high with furniture, bedding, and lamps, and wondered about the future of the hotels. "Everything seemed so solid and permanent," he observed, "that it was impossible to think of the Alcazar as in anything but a state of hibernation. All that seemed necessary was a gentle prod to bring the sleeping giant back to life."

With the end of the war, for a couple of seasons at least, it seemed that the venerable Hotel Ponce de Leon had awakened with a new lease on life. The building and its furnishings were refurbished and a new generation of Americans were invited to relive the glorious days of the Gay Nineties. Indeed, in those quaint days before Disney, such old-time tourist attractions as St. Augustine's Oldest House, Alligator Farm, and Fountain of Youth remained among the state's foremost attractions for sightseers. But long-term prosperity proved illusory, and the house counts resumed a downward spiral. Surveys by the state tourism board explained why: Most tourists were destined for South Florida, most stayed in motels, and many came in the summer months when the hotel was closed. The Flagler hotel company responded in 1958 by opening the Ponce de Leon Motor Lodge north of town next door to the Flagler golf course. The Hotel Ponce de Leon had become superfluous.

Tommy Thompson/Flagler College Archives

THE ALCAZAR REDONE:
THE LIGHTNER MUSEUM AND
THE CITY HALL

The Alcazar took a different path seeking revival. In 1946 Otto C. Lightner of Chicago stayed at the Ponce de Leon and took notice of the boarded-up Alcazar across the way. Lightner was a Midwestern newspaperman who had started *Hobbies* magazine during the Depression and operated a museum in a large Romanesque mansion on Chicago's Michigan Avenue. Lightner was a collector— everything from matchbooks, cigar wrappers, and buttons to Victorian art works being disposed of by wealthy Chicagoans cleaning their parents' attics. He approached the St. Augustine City Commission with an offer to move his museum to the Alcazar. Local leaders were delighted with this opportunity to revitalize "this dark spot in the middle of our city."

Sale of the Alcazar was completed on July 7, 1947. Lightner paid the Florida East Coast Hotel Company $150,000 ($25,000 of which had been raised locally) for the building. It was then immediately handed over to the City of St. Augustine to be held in trust and operated by a self-perpetuating board composed of the mayor and four other prominent citizens.

Lightner immediately started moving his collection down to St. Augustine, one truckload at a time, in the moving van he had purchased. Much of the collection was damaged or stolen in the move. The Alcazar received only superficial alterations to accommodate the museum. The bridge to the Cordova was removed in July 1947. A wooden floor was placed over the Casino's now-empty swimming pool, and dances would be held there after the opening of the museum. Robert Harper, one of Lightner's successors as museum director, wrote in a 1980 history of the museum:

> The newly created Lightner Museum was in many ways two steps backward in what

is now thought of as standard museum exhibition policy. In fact Lightner had at mid-point twentieth century created an almost flawless period piece. The artifacts and their arrangement in the Alcazar displayed many of the cliché conceptions of the typical Victorian museum, but somehow what the Lightner Museum lacked in sophistication it more than equaled in charm. The massing of uncountable quantities of art glass and fine china in immense, poorly labeled cabinets would horrify most museum professionals. Collections of unique, artful and sometimes utilitarian articles on nineteenth century material culture were scattered throughout the maze of former hotel rooms.

Another effort to revitalize the Alcazar was begun in March 1968, when the city commission decided to turn the building into the city hall. The city float-ed a million-dollar bond issue to pay for the renovations. Work began in late 1971 when a wrecking company tore away unneeded parts of the building. In the rear, beside the area which had for-merly been the tennis courts, the utili-ties building and its towering smoke-stack were demolished. The enclosed walkway over the west loggia between the hotel and Casino came down, as did the large dining room that had been added in 1902. A new roof was put over the building, and new windows were installed throughout. The parlor became the city commission meeting room, while the rest of the first floor was uti-lized as municipal office space. The police department moved into the sec-ond floor of the building's east side. However, the rest of the upper floors temporarily remained as empty as they had been in 1932 until city government gradually expanded into them. On April 27, 1973, the new city building was ded-icated. Commissioner James Lindsley declared that St. Augustine now had "the most beautiful, unique, and majes-tic city hall in the nation."

Prior to renovation of the Alcazar into a government building, the artifacts of Lightner Museum had been put into storage. It had been decided to relocate the museum to the Baths area and the Casino, but, due to limited funds, improvements were focused on the Baths. This part of the building was air conditioned, given contemporary lighting, and generally modernized. Fortunately, most of the distinctive fea-

Modern Lightner Ballroom

Lightner Museum

tures of the original interior were retained. The Russian bath changed not at all, and tourists visiting the museum today can sit on the same marble benches where the Bath's patrons sat a century earlier. Finishing touches on the new museum space and the work of unpacking, restoring, and setting up exhibits was done largely by volunteer workers from the community. On the evening of August 12, 1974, Lightner Museum celebrated its rebirth with a formal reception that recalled the elegant social events of Flagler's day.

Finding an adaptive use for the Casino proved difficult. During the American Revolution Bicentennial, thought was given to turning the large space into a community cultural center. Television actor Richard Boone of *Have Gun Will Travel* rigged up a temporary theater on the pool floor and staged the Spanish play *Dog in the Manger* to publicize the effort. However, when a government grant could not be secured for a major project, the pool area became a mall of antique shops and the site of a small café. The ballroom and upper floors evolved into expansion room for the Lightner Museum.

Tommy Thompson/Flagler College Archives

THE PONCE DE LEON REBORN:
FLAGLER COLLEGE

The Alcazar's elder sister, the Hotel Ponce de Leon, experienced a similar miraculous transformation. With the death of William R. Kenan in 1965, the last of the generation that had known Henry Flagler passed away. Lawrence Lewis, Jr., Flagler's principal heir, assumed leadership of Flagler's legacy and developed his own vision for the future of the magnificent old building. On January 18, 1967, he announced that the Hotel Ponce de Leon would close forever at the end of the season. Arrangements had been made to turn the facility into a four-year college for women. This surprise declaration led to an upsurge of visitors, who wanted to stay one last time in the famed hotel. Then in April the hotel closed its doors after eighty momentous seasons.

In September 1968, Flagler College opened to receive the first class of students. It was an inauspicious time. More small, private colleges were closing than opening in the late 1960s. Students moved into the old guest bedrooms, with their outdated furniture, corner fireplaces, and antique bath fixtures. Classes met in the old artists' studios, library shelves filled the Grand Parlor, and the college president set up office in the former ladies' billiard parlor. The first three years of the fledgling school proved to be difficult, but in 1971 Lewis brought in Dr. William Lee Proctor to give Flagler College a fresh start. The college went co-educational and embarked on a long-range expansion program based on conservative financial management, excellence in teaching, and focus on a few academic majors—business, education, liberal arts.

Gradually the old hotel evolved into a true college campus, one with an atmosphere unmatched anywhere. In the early 1980s workers completely gutted the interior of the old utility wing of the hotel and renovated it for classrooms and faculty offices. Shortly thereafter a

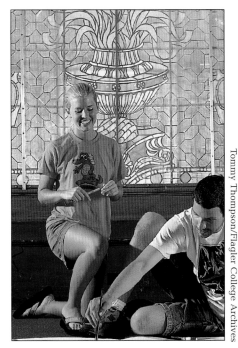

Tommy Thompson/Flagler College Archives

Flagler College students today live and study amid creations by noted artists like Louis C. Tiffany.

team of artists came in to work on a long-term, multi-million-dollar program to restore the wood, plasterwork, Tiffany windows, and Maynard murals. Decades of old faded paint were stripped off walls, which then were repainted to their original colors. In January 1988, Flagler College celebrated the Hotel Ponce de Leon's centennial year with a black-tie dinner. The building had not looked so bright and fresh in a hundred years. Today students sleep and dine where the Rockefellers once tarried.

THE CORDOVA REBORN:
THE NEW CASA MONICA

Flagler's third hotel, the Cordova, vacant since the Great
Depression, was refurbished and reopened in 1968 as the St.
Johns County Courthouse. Most of the interior had been gutted back
to the concrete walls to make space for modern government offices.
The exterior of the hotel's aged gray walls received a coat of plaster
and fresh paint to brighten up appearances.

However, rapid population growth in the 1990s forced the county to abandon the building for a larger facility outside town. Then, in
an amazing reversal of fortune, the former hotel became, once again,
a luxury resort hotel. Richard Kessler, a contemporary entrepreneur
from Orlando, purchased the building in 1997. Again, the building's

interior was radically rearranged. In December 1999, the newly rechristened Casa Monica Hotel registered its first guests in almost seventy years. Arriving visitors could drive their automobiles through the monumental archway that had once been the entrance to Franklin Smith's Plaza del Sol, but which now led to a parking area in the rear of the hotel. Guest apartments were upgraded to the most modern standards. Trendy upscale retailers moved into the row of shops along King Street. The new Casa Monica boasted a first-class restaurant and a banquet room for social occasions. In April of 2001 King Juan Carlos and Queen Sophia of Spain stayed at the Casa Monica while visiting St. Augustine.

The Casa Monica's trademark 1929 Model A stands curbside in front of the beautifully restored hotel.

Tommy Thompson/Flagler College Archives

EPILOGUE

Much has changed since Henry Flagler walked the sandy streets of St. Augustine in 1885 and dreamed of creating a pleasant place for people to spend the winter months. Of course, he could not anticipate the path of future events; yet he built well and left a solid foundation upon which future generations could fashion their own dreams. St. Augustine remains a unique place, blessed by nature and by the wisdom of its most important benefactor. The Memorial Presbyterian Church, Grace Methodist Church, and the Hotels Casa Monica, Alcazar, and Ponce de Leon stand tribute to his vision. The creative new uses of Flagler's fabulous resort hotels have been an effective accommodation to the changes that have taken place in St. Augustine—a graceful blending of history with the present.

SELECT BIBLIOGRAPHY

Extensively annotated versions of the author's research can be found in the following two scholarly articles, from which this book is derived. These articles were also reprinted as pamphlets by the St. Augustine Historical Society.

Thomas Graham, "Flagler's Grand Hotel Alcazar," *El Escribano, The Annual Publication of the St. Augustine Historical Society* (1989), 1–32.

Thomas Graham, "Flagler's Magnificent Hotel Ponce de Leon," *Florida Historical Quarterly* (July 1975), 1–17.

OTHER SOURCES

Akin, Edward. *Flagler: Rockefeller Partner and Florida Baron.* Kent: Kent State University Press, 1988.

Barghini, Sandra. *Henry M. Flagler's Paintings Collection.* Palm Beach: Henry M. Flagler Museum, 2002.

Braden, Susan R. *The Architecture of Leisure: Florida Resort Hotels of Henry Flagler and Henry Plant.* Gainesville: University Presses of Florida, 2002.

Graham, Thomas. *The Awakening of St. Augustine.* St. Augustine: St. Augustine Historical Society, 1978.

Harper, Robert W. "Otto C. Lightner in St. Augustine: The Making of a Museum," *El Escribano, The Annual Publication of the St. Augustine Historical Society* (1980), 59-83.

Martin, Sidney Walter. *Henry Flagler: Visionary of the Gilded Age.* Lake Buena Vista: Tailored Tours, 1998. (Issued under the title *Florida's Flagler* by the University of Georgia Press, 1949, 1977.)

Nolan, David. *Fifty Feet in Paradise: The Booming of Florida.* New York: Harcourt Brace Jovanovich, 1984.

Waterbury, Jean Parker, ed. *The Oldest City: St. Augustine, Saga of Survival.* St. Augustine: St. Augustine Historical Society, 1983.

INDEX

(Illustration page numbers are in boldface.)

If you enjoyed reading this book, here are some other books from Pineapple Press on related topics. For a complete catalog, write to Pineapple Press, P.O. Box 3889, Sarasota, FL 34230 or call 1-800-PINEAPL (746-3275). Or visit our website at www.pineapplepress.com.

Houses of St. Augustine by David Nolan. A history of the city told through its buildings, from the earliest coquina structures, through the colonial and Victorian times, to the modern era. Color photographs and original watercolors. ISBN 1-56164-069-7 (hb), ISBN 1-56164-075-1 (pb)

Ghosts of St. Augustine by Dave Lapham. The unique and often turbulent history of America's oldest city is told in 24 spooky stories that cover 400 years' worth of ghosts. ISBN 1-56164-123-5 (pb)

Oldest Ghosts by Karen Harvey. Read about more St. Augustine ghosts. Includes interviews with people who share their homes with restless spirits. ISBN 1-56164-222-3 (pb)

Florida's Past Volumes 1, 2, and 3 by Gene Burnett. Burnett's easygoing style and his sometimes surprising choice of topics make history good reading in this popular series. **Volume 1** ISBN 1-56164-115-4 (pb); **Volume 2** ISBN 1-56164-139-1 (pb); **Volume 3** ISBN 1-56164-117-0 (pb)

Historic Homes of Florida by Laura Stewart and Susanne Hupp. Seventy-four notable dwellings throughout the state—all open to the public—tell the human side of history. Each is illustrated by H. Patrick Reed or Nan E. Wilson. ISBN 1-56164-085-9 (pb)

The Florida Chronicles by Stuart B. McIver. A series offering true-life sagas of the notable and notorious characters throughout history who have given Florida its distinctive flavor. **Volume 1**: *Dreamers, Schemers and Scalawags* ISBN 1-56164-155-3 (pb); **Volume 2**: *Murder in the Tropics* ISBN 1-56164-079-4 (hb); **Volume 3**: *Touched by the Sun* ISBN 1-56164-206-1 (hb)

Florida Portrait by Jerrell Shofner. Packed with hundreds of photos, this word-and-picture album traces the history of Florida from the Paleoindians to the rampant growth of the late twentieth century. ISBN 1-56164-121-9 (pb)

Art Lover's Guide to Florida by Anne Jeffrey and Aletta Dreller. Tour 86 of the most dynamic and exciting art groupings in Florida. Brilliant color photos. ISBN 1-56164-144-8 (pb)

Bansemer's Book of Florida Lighthouses by Roger Bansemer. This beautiful book depicts Florida's 30 lighthouses in over 200 paintings and sketches. ISBN 1-56164-172-3 (hb)